SPIRITUALITY WITHOUT STRUCTURE

An erudite and cogent introduction to a complex subject written with all the clarity we have come to expect from this remarkable writer.
Graeme Talboys

I give this nonfiction work five stars, for being a cool goblet of spiritual refreshment – and for actually being literally refreshing – and not some dry heaving clichéd gibberish that the real people making up the population couldn't possibly understand. I think the Author has found her calling, and I am glad to have found myself called.
C.H. Scarlett

The author is extremely knowledgeable in her field, and very accomplished in getting her view and ideas across to the reader. The book, as well as being extremely well written, is detailed and in depth without being overcomplicated or laborious to read. It is very well researched, incredibly interesting and thought provoking. A real must for all those who are interested in religion and beliefs, be they Druid, Christian or Atheist, anyone with an open and keen mind will get something out of reading it.
Amy Cummins (Hellbound Media and The Great Escape)

I see your book as an encouragement to feel not only comfortable, but excited about not following a religion. It provides the stimulus for us to start building our own philosophy, our own sense of ~~~ own spiritual way…
Phillip Carr Gomm

T0167614

PAGAN PORTALS

Spirituality Without Structure

The power of Finding
Your Own Path

Pagan Portals

Spirituality Without Structure

The power of Finding
Your Own Path

Nimue Brown

MOON
BOOKS

Winchester, UK
Washington, USA

First published by Moon Books, 2013
Moon Books is an imprint of John Hunt Publishing Ltd., Laurel House, Station Approach,
Alresford, Hants, SO24 9JH, UK
office1@jhpbooks.net
www.johnhuntpublishing.com
www.moon-books.net

For distributor details and how to order please visit the 'Ordering' section on our website.

Text copyright: Nimue Brown 2013

ISBN: 978 1 78279 280 2

A CIP catalogue record for this book is available from the British Library.

Design and cover: Stuart Davies

Printed and bound by CPI Group (UK) Ltd, Croydon, CR0 4YY

We operate a distinctive and ethical publishing philosophy in all
areas of our business, from our global network of authors to
production and worldwide distribution.

CONTENTS

Acknowledgements

Atheist author Alain de Botton and Christian heretic Mark Townsend have been significant inspirations to me of late. Both gentlemen demonstrate that a person can be inside a thing and not ruled by it. Alain de Botton is clearly not interested in the usual atheist game of bashing the believers, but wants some kind of spirituality rooted in life, that gives soul and meaning to an absence of belief in a monotheistic God. Partly I've written in response to his words. Mark is a follower of Jesus, who has been inside the institution of the Church and demonstrated through his life and work that a person can belong to a religion without submitting to its politics.

Thank you Philip Carr-Gomm and Graeme Talboys for words of encouragement.

I'd like to thank my husband Tom Brown for the exquisite cover, which he made before the book was written. Seeing it caused me to want to write something worthy of the art, and that was a real spur to deeper thinking.

Finally, a deep bow to the one person without whom this book simply would not exist. Trevor Greenfield is a most excellent publisher and an ongoing source of both hope and inspiration to me. He is everything an author would want in a publisher, and so I dedicate this book to him, with heartfelt thanks for everything he's done, both for me, and for Pagan writing as a whole.

Introduction

This is a book for people who have given up on formal religious systems, or want to, and are wondering where that leaves them. It's often a confusing space to find yourself in. There isn't even an agreed terminology to describe what you are doing. Some who step away from religion may identify with philosophies, or New Age thinking, some may hang on to elements of religions whilst wanting to do their own thing. Others build from scratch. No matter where you come from, trying to find your own alternative to religion will bring you to a commonality of issues faced by others who work in the same way. For convenience, I'm going to abbreviate this kind of questing down to the term 'own path' as being a functional, descriptive term.

Own path practice is full of challenges and, by definition, lacking in wider support networks, so this book aims to offer some ways of thinking about how to go it alone. Many people yearn to be spiritual without wanting to be tied into a formal practice; simply knowing that you aren't the only one can be very helpful.

I'm not making any assumptions about the beliefs of potential readers. I think if a thing is going to work, it needs to be as viable for as many people as possible. Thus I'm writing with an eye to atheists, polytheists, agnostics and people of monotheistic faith alike. The things that draw us to religions are human, the things we need from a spiritual life are human, and I've come to the conclusion that what we believe about the presence, absence or nature of deity is the least important thing in terms of how we practice. From a personal perspective, belief or the absence thereof might well feel like the most important thing. It can be incredibly divisive. If we step away from the issue of belief and look more about what religion is and does, what spirituality means, what the human issues are, then we can find commonality and make better sense of things. That said, I am a Pagan, and a lot of my ideas come from my experience of contemporary Paganism. I'm writing from what I know, and at times that may well colour things.

It may seem odd to find the author of two books on Druidry writing a rejection of structured religion, but in essence that's what I'm poised to do. Some explanation seems appropriate, so here goes... I've been an informal student of religion ever since taking a module in the subject at college. Most academics focus on studying one religion, but it's always been the inter-religion work that fascinates me. Comparative religion shows us so much about what people do at deeper levels. There is so much commonality between faiths. That similarity comes in part from long histories of cross-pollination, but also occurs because the aspects of life that drive us towards wanting religions are themselves universal. We live, we die, and we wonder about it. In this book I'm drawing on a wide reading base across different religions, and contact with people of faiths. Given the shortness of the book there's a lot of generalising and I've not referenced much, but most of the content is not obscure and anyone curious can readily follow through on what I've observed here. The only insight that is not easily replicated comes from my years as a Pagan volunteer. Many people come to Paganism because they have rejected the religion they were brought up in. The process and implications of that rejection, and the reasons for it have been frequent topics of conversation for me. I've learned a lot about what disenchants people, as a consequence, and also what it is that people yearn for in their spiritual lives. I also find myself attracted to atheists, fascinated by the absolute logic, and the occasional bouts of what I see as illogical fundamentalism that so often goes with that perspective. Atheism as a whole has been a large influence, considering the ways in which it does act as a substitute for religion, and the things it proves unequal to. I acknowledge a huge debt to Alain de Botton, whose wonderful book *Religion for Atheists* set me down the track of really considering what religion means.

Personal experience has also fed into writing this book. I grew up in a loosely Pagan household, attending a Church of England primary school, and was exposed to all kinds of traditions along the way. Even as a child I knew I couldn't do belief, but was drawn to nature religions and their mythologies all the same. For a time I felt myself to be a sort of agnostic Pagan. I acquired the popular and largely meaningless term 'general eclectic Pagan' thanks to The Pagan Federation. Then I found Druidry, and settled there. It's such a diverse tradition that a person's beliefs, or absence thereof, are very much their own business. Meeting atheist Druids, I was inspired by their ideas, and ways of relating to the world. Over the years I've found my own path, and it has been very much shaped by doubt and uncertainty. The only thing I believe is that there is no one true way.

Atheist humanism shows us that what we do in our lives ought to make sense in compassionate, human terms, ideally. It's the only measuring tool we have and should replace any ideas about what Gods allegedly want us to do. Reality can fall a long way short of prioritising compassion, and formal religions especially so. It seems that the more fundamentalist a religion becomes, the less compassionate it is. The more doubt we hold, the more likely we are to treat each other gently. Doubt appears to be a lot kinder than certainty when it comes to matters of faith.

I've read enough history books to know that the relationship between religion and politics is often strong and seldom benefits the majority. Opium of the people would be less of a problem than what we get, perhaps. Religion is the means by which countless lives have been harnessed, saddled and sent forth to suit a private or political agenda. Religions accumulate wealth, power and the means to tell people what to do. This makes them attractive to tyrants. I'm too anarchic, too opposed to authority and oppression to have any sympathy for this process, and am angry about the ways in which innocent faiths are subverted for the gain of the few.

Spirituality should uplift us, not keep us materially powerless and downtrodden. Every phrase that celebrates noble poverty and the good of suffering helps to perpetuate poverty and suffering. This is not compassionate humanity, but it is very convenient for the rich and powerful who wish to hang on to their advantages. There are a lot of political undercurrents in this book. The history of religion is political, the act of stepping away from formal religions has political implications, and these need considering. Religion and state are never truly separate because our beliefs inform our choices. The beliefs of those in power inform their choices too.

What I've tried to do with this little book, is to pick apart the differences between spirituality as experienced by the individual, and religion as a formal system of control. While I have considerable respect for sincere people of all faiths, I take issue with the effects of religious systems. The ideas I have to offer are as applicable to atheists as to people of conventional faith, because both of these positions can lend themselves to a genuine spiritual outlook. I'm writing predominantly for the many people who are rejecting systems and striking out on their own. Nonetheless I suspect it is my fellow Pagans who will enjoy this the most. The very nature of Paganism tends to reject attempts at authority. There are as many forms of Paganism as there are Pagans, it is inherently an 'own-path' practice.

I have not offered any solutions here, just ways of raising questions that might be helpful to someone who is trying to figure out how to be spiritual on their own terms. I've identified what it is that religion does and what we might want spirituality to give us, and how we might go about looking for those things. My primary argument is that the only way to be spiritual is to do it on your own terms – anything else is subservience. This is a book written for you to dismantle, borrow from, reject bits of, reinvent and otherwise play with. It is not any kind of alternate authority and the author would be delighted if you made free with the contents in any way that helps you find your own path.

Why Paganism Mostly isn't a Religion

Plenty of people who are not Pagans seem to think it is a single, coherent religion with all the usual trappings: books, temples, founders, leaders, structures, rules and order. This can cause some confusion. Even within Paganism, people seem to think Druids are all organised and like the Church, which is a long way wide of the mark. There are times when Pagans (and for that matter, Druids) find it easier to go along with this. For one thing, not everyone has the time or inclination for a proper explanation.

The most obvious point to make is that Paganism is not 'a religion' but a passably useful way of lumping together a likeminded minority. There are benefits to be derived from speaking with one voice, or being recognised as a group. There are many traditions within Paganism – Witches, Druids, Heathens, Shamans, Hellenics, Dianics, Kemeticists, Religio Romano, to name a few of the more obvious ones. There are a great many eclectics and own-path folk as well. Taken as individual groups, none of the sub-groups within Paganism are big enough to speak productively to government and the like. The grouping under a shared 'Pagan' banner has served us politically and in handling the media, but is better understood as a pressure group than as any kind of organised religion.

Even the above breakdown into major subgroups is misleading. There are plenty of people who identify across those lines, and who also connect with other religions. There are significant numbers of Christian Pagans and Pagan Buddhists, along with pretty much any other cross pollination you can think of. To further complicate things, subgroups can be divided up into sets that can be significantly different from each other. Druids can be animists, polytheists and non-theists. Alternatively you might look at revivalists, reconstructionists and neo-Druids. You could divide along the lines of Irish Druidry, Welsh, French and non-

European, or further divide by country. Each has its own view of Druids, and many Druids are not in Orders. Some orders are more demanding of conformity than others. Druidry is not a single, coherent religion any more than Christianity is, once you get beneath the surface. However, in our case, the divisions are frequently arbitrary and tend to depend on your reasons for wanting to clump people into groups in the first place.

We could divide up any of the Pagan subgroups in this way, breaking Paganism down into ever smaller religions. Start dealing with individual Pagans and you'll find exceedingly individual definitions of path: Welsh Druid, Kitchen Witch, Celtic Shaman, Witchidruid, Polytheistic Bardic Druid, Brythonic reconstructionist. There are probably more kinds of Paganism than there are living Pagans to embody it all. There is a lot of commonality between these many labels and ways of practising, just as there is between the many subsets of other religions. When you compare Mormons, Catholics, Methodists and Jehovah's Witnesses, as a small subset of Christian diversity, it's clear that you can squeeze a lot of variety under one religious heading. However, in most defined religions, there's also a defined focus of worship and some core features in common, and we do not have those. Here are some of the key things we might be expected to hold in common were Paganism to be a single religion.

1. A core text that we hold sacred. (Also absent in Shinto, although we do have ancient Pagan texts for some paths.)
2. A named founder like Jesus, Abraham or Mohammed. (Shinto has no named founder and the modern witches have Gerald Gardner and Alex Saunders, arguably. Polytheistic religions tend to put less emphasis on founders than monotheism does.)
3. A set of core rules. (Many paths have their own ethical guidelines, but those do not deliver hard and fast 'thou shalts' that conform to other people's expectation of what

ethics should look like.)

4. A single agreed opinion about the nature of deity, life after death or the meaning of life. (There can be more coherence within subgroups, but even here ideas can vary a lot. We may be unique in this.)

5. Some kind of earthly leader of the faithful. (There is no leader of Pagans, nor do any of the major subgroups have a 'Pope' equivalent. Jainism and Shinto have no leadership in this style either.)

6. Financial structures and property. (Any financial arrangements are at a very local level, which is also true of Jainism and Shinto.)

7. Converts. (This tends to be a monotheistic issue. Most traditional religions that relate to culture and heritage have no interest in cultures, so Judaism, Jainism and Shinto do not recruit either.)

8. Physical structures to worship in. (Ancient Pagans had temples, but for the greater part we do not own our spaces and do it outside. Plenty of other groups have managed with less formal meeting spaces at times in their history too.)

This list covers the external trappings and actions that can easily be seen by those considering a religion from the outside. Thus while many may assume Paganism is a lot like everything else, on closer investigation there are plenty who will decide that it isn't a 'proper' religion at all because it lacks these obvious features. The 'not a proper religion' argument is popular with those who wish to denigrate and disempower. However, given that there are two internationally recognised religions – Jainism and Shinto – that also lack a lot of the external trappings, this seems at best a poor excuse for prejudice. There is a lot more to spiritual coherence than structure. Our wider culture's tendency to emphasise superficial structure can make us oblivious to the far more important issues of what a religious group actually does in the world.

It is possible to discard the idea of religions as buildings and sacred books, and to consider them in terms of how they function and what they do. This both sheds an interesting light on more established religion and gives room for Paganism and other less structured faiths, in the process. Much of the time in this book I'm trying to step back and ask what religion does, and what spirituality does, and what the differences mean.

When we consider the activities of Pagans, we can bring to the table the undertaking of ritual, rites of passage, prayer and celebration. These are clear manifestations of spirituality and, arguably, of religion. Paganism has community and service aspects like many religions, there are teaching aspects, and there is an informal priesthood. We have a great deal that is spiritual in nature, and far less of the physical baggage that has attached itself to most standard religions in the past two thousand years or so. It would be tempting to argue that what we do is in fact older and more authentic. It is certainly more real.

Critics on the outside of Paganism will often suggest that a lack of the usual trappings mean a lack of depth. The flip side of this is that those same trappings can make it easy to go through the motions without doing anything remotely spiritual, uplifting or meaningful. The person who has no standard forms to fall back on, is obliged to invent and discover as they go and has no choice but to live their path. Such an approach demands relevance to the world we live in, requires responsibility and necessitates independent thinking.

There are groups within Paganism that choose or have fallen into fixed practice, come up with settled ritual and magical methods, adopted fixed prayers or otherwise landed in a groove. Anyone wanting and finding one of these more structured manifestations can of course treat it exactly like a regular religion. If you want an authority to turn to, a source of direction and the like, there are groups that can give you this. You can find codes, laws and required reading lists, clothing regulations and all of that structure. However, this is a complex and nuanced business, its precise functioning having everything to do with the people involved.

Individuals who want rules and a guru will find them, whether they were offered or not. In Monty Python's 'The Life of Brian', Brian loses a sandal whilst fleeing from a crowd. They take this as a sign that they are also to remove the left sandal. That's a subset of religious people in a nutshell. If you want that from Paganism, you can find or fabricate it. Outside of comedy films, this is a dull and unrewarding way to go. That which is understood is always so much more powerful than that which is merely accepted.

It is possible to enter fairly structured spaces and not be ruled by them. With its three levels of training, ritual designs and graded attire, The Order of Bards, Ovates and Druids would seem at a first glance to be a bastion of structure. Those who go there seeking structures seem to find what they need. I'm a chaotic creature by nature, and went simply to learn. I found most of the formal bits were optional, there's no requirement to regurgitate any of it, and that I could learn and use what I found to develop my own practice with the support of my tutors. I found what I wanted to find, and I think we often do.

There's a lot of difference between an enabling structure, and power for the sake of it. People who want authority turn up in all religions and are easy to spot because they go around telling people what to think and how to feel. Authority needs to enforce itself. Sadly there are often desperately fragile egos in the mix, craving the reassurance that comes when no one argues with you. There are others who seek fame, power, status and wealth and simply see religion as a means to those ends. All too often, formal religions are not the enabling structures we might want them to be, but are instead corrupted by individual and corporate desires for power.

As human beings we seem to find strong leadership enticing. We like it when someone else takes the risks, makes the decision, solves the problems and tells us what to do. Religions can be very good at matching those who wish to graze quietly with those who wish to be shepherds. It is also worth remembering that you can just as easily match those who do not want to make much effort with the kind of shepherd who runs a very lucrative abattoir.

It is important to know yourself. Are you looking for comfort, a sense of security, some rules to follow, a nice plan for the afterlife and a routine? If so, then stay with regular religions and structures. If, on the other hand, you want spiritual experiences and to find your own answers, are not afraid to take risks, face setbacks and ask a lot of questions, then doing as you are told is never going to satisfy you.

This book is all about breaking out and doing it for yourself. I'll admit I have an agenda here. I think there is much to be troubled by in people who want power over other people, and over other aspects of the natural world. I believe the desire for power is driven by fear and that it is inherently destructive. I also believe that we do best when we seek harmony, tolerance and collaboration, and when we respect each other as equals. As soon as you try to control another person, you diminish them, and yourself.

The structure of religion is so often about control. There are too many issues around who has the right to make whom do what. The right to punish, to exile, own and to devalue can all be tied up in religious thinking too, and these are destructive influences across the globe. I'm much more interested in the power to control the self, and the self-discipline that is all about what happens inside an individual.

The trouble with having no structure or system – as is so often the case for independent modern Pagans – is ascertaining what you might replace that with. Figuring everything out from scratch is rewarding, and a profound journey in its own right, but you may have to start by working out what to work out in the first place and this can lead to a great deal of wheel re-invention. It is possible to learn a lot from the history and diversity of religion – Pagan and non-Pagan alike. We can learn without subscribing to any one system, drawing inspiration without abdicating personal power. I'm not suggesting a 'pick and mix' attitude to spirituality, but a process of stepping back to examine what religion is and does. We can learn from the areas of overlap and commonality. We can learn from the places of difference and conflict. I've gathered together much of what I've learned from reading about different religions and listening to a great many people. This is not the whole story. It's not even the tip of one. The drive for spirituality in humans and the history of religion are two vast topics that it would probably take lifetimes to understand. However, the attempt is always worth it and I hope this provides a useful jumping off point.

The Limitations of Standard Religion

The UK census of 2011 showed a significant drop since 2001 –
13% – of people identifying as Christians. There are around
30,000 atheists, 30,000 agnostics, and the number of people
claiming 'no religion' is on the rise, as are the various forms of
Paganism.[1] The move away from traditional religion in this
country is growing, and while Christians remain the majority,
culturally we can no longer assume Christianity as a natural
default. How many people within Christianity are part of a
religious system and how many are more independent, is
another question, but not all who claim to be Christian are
following a system dictated to them by others anymore. Formal
religion in this country no longer has the political force behind it
to make it mandatory. Any religion that depends on legal force to
maintain its membership, is not essentially about anything
spiritual. Where religion moves away from force and power, it
becomes more meaningful. If spirituality is a matter of soul, it
cannot, by any reasonable understanding of what those words
mean, be forced upon a person. This is as relevant an issue when
considering the Taliban, as it is in the controlling desires of right
wing Christian America.

When religious leaders express prejudice against women –
who still aren't allowed to be bishops, and still have no status in
other religions too, that's half the population potentially
alienated. Gay and lesbian people continue to be denigrated by
mainstream religion, and it is little wonder if they seek elsewhere
for meaningful spiritual engagement. Human and compassionate behaviour does not exclude on these terms, but the traditional systems of religion are often laden with intolerance.

The books and rules of structured religions come from times
so distant from our own as to be alien. What made sense in
distant lands, thousands of years ago, has no ready application

to modern life. Much of it makes no sense. The process of trying to wrap old thinking around new problems causes all kinds of difficulties, and tends to result in a loss of relevance. Either you leave the old behind, in which case you have lost the system, or you reinterpret what you do have and rely on modern human rethinks of what was supposedly divine thinking, or the inspiration of a great leader. Whichever way you go, something vital is bound to be lost. Who has a neighbour with an ass, much less reason to covet it? But, 'Do not envy your neighbour's car,' just doesn't carry the same ring of age and significance.

While for some, the structures supply comfort, stability and a sense of meaning, increasing numbers of people struggle with issues of relevance. Science has reduced our need for supernatural explanations. The power, wealth and inevitable corruption that feature in all huge organisations seem wholly at odds with any notion of spirituality. As that becomes ever more visible through the media, it becomes less tolerated. The way in which the Catholic Church protected paedophile priests is a prime example of the kind of behaviour which compromises structured religion in many people's eyes. The business-like nature of Jehovah's Witnesses and Scientologists smells more like capitalism than enlightenment. The same could be said of many monstrously expensive New Age interventions.

A glance at history shows us much to be uneasy about, with political power casting a baleful influence over religious practice. Holy wars, religiously endorsed tyrants, suicide bombers and martyrs show an alarmingly inhuman face to religious bodies. While there are many religious individuals who deserve every respect, there's frequently something unhealthy about religious structures. Perhaps it is simply that structures themselves breed hierarchies and tend to accumulate money. This makes religion attractive to people who seek power and money. Religion is often just another excuse to do as you will. It delivers an ideological structure that can carry the people in your power into war, oppression, death and madness. Here I think Shinto is an important example. A land-based, soulful spirituality, Shinto was utilised for politics during the Second World War, leading to Kamikaze pilots. The Kami in Shinto, are benevolent spirits of harmony and peace, Kamikaze is a horrible subversion to serve a brutal agenda. No wonder that for many people, the only answer is to retreat from all such systems. A church of one has little scope for corruption, but it is lonely.

I was deeply inspired by Alain de Botton's *Religion for Atheists*. This book considers the social and psychological functions of religion and tries to reclaim the good bits for atheists. I've been tussling with similar issues for a long time: I am a spiritual person, but I'm also a rationalist, and lousy at belief. I can't easily believe in that which I do not experience. I live in a culture that defines old-style religious experience (seeing lights, hearing voices, burning bushes speaking to you) as expressions of madness. That makes me cautious about seeking certain kinds of experience for myself. I also have to wonder about the historical relationship between religious experience and madness. Is it simply the case that the inspiration underpinning ancient, sacred texts is a product of poor mental health? Could this simply be the schizophrenia of our ancestors? At the same time, I don't want to take my doubt and caution to the other extreme, ruling out everything I have no first-hand experience of. I've never seen Australia, but am pretty sure it exists.

Rationality demands that we recognise the limitations of our senses, sciences and measuring tools. Even in science, there are always more questions than answers, and this year's trusted tool is bound to be replaced by something else in the future.

This is a small book about how to be spiritual without being at the mercy of religious systems. How to be a thinking and feeling person, rational, doubting and still open to the numinous. We are so collectively used to the idea of religious systems and structures being the norm, that alternative and own-path folk can encounter a lot of wry smiles and gentle mockery. Sometimes not so gentle. I want to offer both a reasoned defence of the importance of own-path practice, and some non-dogmatic ideas as a framework in which a lone traveller can place themselves. This is not a structure. It's not a map. This is a method for making your own map, building your own compass and ascertaining your direction.

Systems, structures, buildings and hierarchies are not intrinsic to spirituality. They aren't even necessary, but have become so entangled in how we think about religion as to be mistaken for it. These are all outward shows that can be expressions of belief, but can equally be about conformity, control, lip service and habit. It is vitally important to distinguish between heartfelt spirituality, and everything else. If exploring spirituality ultimately takes you back to certain texts, ideals or activities, that's fine. What matters here is the integrity of what you do, its relevance to you, and the choices you make.

It's also worth pointing out that you can have recognisable religions without having the trappings we've come to associate all too often with that word. Jainism is non-theistic, and has no hierarchy structure and no formal priesthood. It functions both socially and spiritually as an internationally recognised religion, without having the things in religions that are so often barriers to spirituality. Many Pagan groups eschew structures as well. It can be done, and a lot of people do it.

Spirituality is a Felt Thing

Whatever your focus, spiritual practice should not be about meaningless ritual repetition. It should not be merely a habit or a means of appeasing others. Nor should spirituality be a wholly intellectual exercise. There is a significant place for thinking and philosophy, and I will return to explore that later on, but spiritual experience has to be grounded in feeling. The emotional impact of what we do is what moves us and takes us forward, and it is the emotional experience that is the most rewarding. Without it, we're just going through the motions. There are religious writers from various traditions who offer submission to God as the only goal of religion. By this assessment, what you feel is explicitly considered irrelevant; obedience is everything. To me, this makes a total nonsense of spirituality. Blind obedience to that which does not expose us to mystery, or feed the soul, is just blind obedience. So often this combines with serving someone else's agenda. This is one of the primary things I wish to challenge. We have no real evidence for the existence of deity, only personal experience. Anyone seeking deity must, surely, look to personal experience to be doing anything other than following some other person's unfounded instructions? Where we blindly follow the instructions of others, we become desperately vulnerable to abuse and manipulation.

Even if you accept that book religions are founded on the revealed word of deity, it is important to acknowledge the human influence in the process. Humans have written those words down, copied, translated, and often interpreted. Decisions are made about which texts to include and which to reject. At the very least, this indisputable human element must make the writing less than divine perfection. We should not treat as pristine and divine that which has grubby human fingerprints all over it.

It is my impression that humans have made up the stories in the first place, too. They may be inspired, but they are intrinsically human. Stories are good and useful things, right up to the point where some other human demands you place blind faith in them, treat them as literal truths and act accordingly. We have used stories in this way through human history to justify the obscene and to quash rational and compassionate thinking.

It is one thing to devote time to a practice or idea to see what develops, accepting that it may not work right off. It is quite another thing to keep repeating an activity you have established isn't working for you, in the hopes that it will either change, or score you points with the supernatural. Failure to find meaning can be written off as a consequence of doing it wrong, being insufficiently pious, impatient, or a hundred other dispiriting things. Finding the line between necessary patience and pointlessness is not automatic, and we should expect to have to work at things sometimes. If a practice doesn't resonate with you, or make sense, it may simply be wrong for you. When religions require actions that seem irrational, feel wrong or don't make you feel anything at all, there's every chance it was never about spiritual experience. I've even had Druid practitioners tell me that I must repeat meditations that don't work for me, and repeat them daily because they are necessary. To question that, was, I was told, to disrespect both the teacher and the tradition. This kind of attitude is a barrier to spirituality, not a tool. It is about the authority of the one making demands. Human desires for power and control need guarding against in spiritual work. It should always be possible to question, to adapt practice or seek a viable alternative at the very least.

Anything that frustrates, or makes you feel silly takes you away from spiritual experience, not towards it. Self consciousness, feelings of absurdity and so forth tend towards disempowerment and disengage you. It's off-putting and few of us respond well to feeling humiliated. But, what is a spiritual experience? Structured religions will often tell you what to do, but not what to be looking for as a consequence of the undertaking. What does a spiritual experience feel like? How can you tell if you've had one? Clearly, God is not going to appear in a burning bush for everyone. If you don't even believe in anything supernatural in the first place, is spiritual experience even possible? It is. It can come almost anywhere, and to anyone. We all have different triggers. I find my spiritual moments in the flight of an egret, pristine against a grey winter sky, and in the flows of inspiration, to give two examples. For others, it might be found in the ecstasy of dance, the energy of a sports crowd or the solitude of deep contemplation. There are many ways, and a lot of them do not depend on standard religious practice.

A spiritual experience gives a person a feeling of profound connection with something beyond themselves. That something doesn't have to be a god. It could be a place, a person, a tradition, or an idea. Anything, potentially, can be connected with. The spiritual experience breaks down the isolation of self, deepening a feeling of involvement, it gives an emotional sense of meaning, significance or elevation. For some practitioners, this also breaks down notions of identity, and for others, it doesn't. Reliably though, this connectedness feels like a force for good. It is an uplifting, inspiring and positive occurrence that may last for seconds or far longer. This in turn may well inspire feelings of love, hope, compassion and the like within the individual. In feeling this way, the person can also receive the impression that the same positive effects are coming to them from outside, that love and hope are bestowed by some external force. This can be literally true if your spiritual moments connect you to other people. Holding that all important doubt, it may, or may not represent a literal truth the rest of the time, but either way the psychological consequences are real.

The final consequence of a spiritual experience is a sense of the numinous. This can manifest within us as awe, wonder, terror, ecstasy, or potentially any other intense emotion. There is an overwhelming quality to it, and a keen sense of contacting something bigger than the individual. This may open a door to existential fear (an issue I shall return to later) which is often a vital part of the spiritual journey. The numinous can also provide creative and life inspiration. No matter how it manifests, one of the ways we can identify it, is that it leaves a mark. To experience the numinous is to be changed. That which does not change us in any way may be interesting and significant, but it isn't numinous.

Traditional western thinking categorises religious experience as rare, unpredictable and not actually necessary for the religious life. Normal thinking often views the numinous as a fleeting thing, and the transience is part of what normally defines it as a religious experience in the first place. Eastern traditions tend to see religious experience as a journey into deeper relationship, not as an event – a perspective I favour. It is also my experience that the numinous can be actively sought in all things, that it can become a part of life, that you can build a sense of how to find it and that it is absolutely essential to spirituality, and for that matter, to being human. Religious systems that devalue the individual quest for numinous experience deny humanity one of the most profound experiences available. Moving into a deeper religious or spiritual experience of life is profoundly rewarding and has the power to illuminate and make meaningful everything that we do. Why would anyone want to make that seem hard, or irrelevant?

If we could all reach out to the numinous for ourselves, we would not need religious structures. The life blood cash flows would reduce, if not dry up entirely. Why pay to be told about a mystery you are also told you cannot approach, if you know exactly how to find and experience it for yourself? There are wider political aspects to this issue as well. We spend a lot of money distracting ourselves with a vast array of commercial products that offer us no wonder and no soul nourishment. How would our politics, our consumer habits, our relationships with everything change, if we all had access to the numinous? For those mired in materialism, anyone else rejecting it has the potential for disaster.

The quest for spiritual experience begins with the quest for feeling. What moves you? Has anything in your life been beautiful enough to make you cry? What took your breath away, put you on your knees with awe, turned your world over and shook it? Those are the keys. Follow those things, seek and court them, make space in your life for them and treat whatever moves you as vitally important. Honour it, by whatever means makes sense. The rest will come in its own time.

There is a theory that tried and tested methods of religions are reliable ways to the divine. Follow the instructions and, if you are good enough, you can expect results. For some people, this seems to work nicely. However, it is the inspiration derived from the system, from belief, or a resonance in the practice that really makes the difference here. Repeating actions that leave you cold and fail to inspire, is unlikely to reveal the numinous. The same approaches do not work for everyone, which is why religions used to try to engage people on many different levels. Music, art, theology, architecture, ritual, poetry, drama and even taste are part of the traditional religious experience. Religions used to be centres for and sponsors of creativity. Where religions have focused more on the thinking and less on sensory impact, it's easy for people to become less engaged. Take the creativity out of religion and you also take away much of its capacity to inspire.

If you have yet to be deeply touched by life, the process may take a bit longer, but is entirely available to you. Sometimes it's just a matter of broadening your experience, exploring new things until you find something resonant or inspiring enough to take you further. Modern cultures teach us to suppress our emotions and we can end up hiding feelings from ourselves as well as others. Permission to feel can be an important first step. Being open to your own emotions is necessary if you are seeking spiritual experience. Do not rule out the rush that comes with intellectual achievement, though. Some emotions are a bit more cerebral than others. Whether you feel it between your ears, in the pit of your stomach or in your reproductive organs, it all counts as feeling, and it all has the potential to show you wonder.

The experience of beauty can be an easy way of letting something external move and inspire you. This is a good step towards experiencing the numinous. The natural world, from a lone urban tree to an epic sweep of landscape, offers beauty in abundance. Sunsets are a frequent display of overwhelming wonder. The enormity of the universe, hinted at in a night sky, is there to be experienced. In life and death, pain and love, in the compassion and cruelty of fellow humans, daily life offers a stream of miracles. Most of the trick lies in starting to notice these wonders. Then it is a case of letting them act upon you, and taking seriously your felt response to the experience. Make room for this. Sit with it when you can. Let it inspire you. The numinous is all around us, waiting to be found.

Religious systems ask you to take up their methods regardless of the results. The focus then is not your experience, but your willingness to submit. The carrot of possible experience may be dangled, but often remains out of reach. Religions do not require you to have private spiritual experience. Someone else can mediate that on your behalf, so long as you jump through the right hoops in the right ways. You can feel grateful for the meditation and the promise of things beyond your grasp. To be in a religious context and unable to feel what is supposedly happening, is an alienating process, or a demoralizing one. Veneration of the system at the expense of personal experience, is all about the system.

There is no call for belief in the quest for wonder, nor do you need to ascribe supernatural meaning to what happens. The most rational and non-believing person can still feel awe. Whether it is the beauty of a mathematical equation, a rainbow or a melody, these things simply exist. All you have to do is encounter something that causes an emotional response within you. No gods are necessary, just your attention.

Build Your Own Philosophy

Philosophy is the language, tools, traditions and habits of thinking about stuff, in essence. It can be understood in terms of both evolving traditions, and as an activity. The philosophical aspects of religions are not always self-announcing, but they are always a consideration. Buddhism and Taoism clearly express themselves as being more philosophical than religious in nature. However, even when philosophy is not proclaimed, it still exists. Every religious system has an attitude, or a set of attitudes to all the big questions of life, the universe and everything. Some of them hold together better than others, some can seem contra-dictory. Joseph Campbell in *The Power of Myth*[2] suggests that religious rules are about how we treat fellow members of the tribe, not outsiders. It may be that apparent contradictions owe a lot to taking systems out of their original context, but for a modern practitioner, there are no tidy solutions to apparent contradictions in these underlying ideas.

Beneath the rituals, prayers and parables, behind the altars and underpinning the temples, are assumptions about how the world works. There are attitudes to what life and death means. We can learn what, from a given perspective, the point of life is supposed to be, and how we should consequently live. Assumption and belief, not just in deity, but in the whole nature of living and being, underpin religious systems. What does it mean to be human? What does it take to be a good person? What is the difference between right and wrong? How should we respond to other people's wrongs?

However, more problematically, part of the philosophy of religious systems tends to be the belief that the system itself is not merely right, but perfect beyond questioning. The under-pinning philosophy is not to be questioned. Attempts at dealing with the illogical or unreasonable will bring you straight back to the will of god and the wisdom of the ancients. If you argue, you are just going to be wrong.

Religions do not tend to invite doubt or query of their underlying assumptions. You can talk about the number of angels on a pinhead or the best way to pray, or what direction you might pray to if you were in space, but these are all relatively superficial. Perhaps, in the schools and hierarchies some religions have places where even the underpinnings can be considered, but for your average practitioner, questioning the very authority of the religion in this way is never going to get much encouragement. The system depends on being an unassailable system in the first place. Question its absolute authority, and the entire foundation starts to wobble.

Faith is, by its nature, rooted in the idea that religious doctrines represent divine truth. However, once you start thinking about religions in term of their philosophies, it is a lot easier to deconstruct the authority and look at it for what it does, not what it claims to be.

If you are interested in building a path from scratch, a philosophy will be necessary to you. This is the point at which intellect is brought into the issue of spirituality. Intellect is not at odds with the quest for a more spiritual awareness and can be a very powerful tool in developing yourself.

Like 'religion', 'philosophy' is a word that evokes a feeling of rules, structures and authority. Here, the gatekeepers are academic, while the sheer size and weight of the Western tradition can be intimidating. It is possible to be a philosophical person without being wholly immersed in the often impenetrable available texts. What philosophy has done, from the most ancient humans onwards, is to ask questions that could not easily be answered. Why are we here? What does it all mean? How does one live well? Is this the best of all possible worlds? What comes first, ideas, or things? Some questions may seem more relevant than others. Where philosophy has practical applications, the subject has fed into and been replaced by the sciences. Consequently much of the older writing, pre-science, is of limited relevance to the person on their own path. Where academic philosophy gets too abstract or obsessed with making up a solid story about ultimately unknowable things, it can feel a bit pointless.

A personal philosophy is a whole other thing from this kind of academic philosophy. It does not require that you engage with any existent philosophical tradition, unless you want to. In this way personal philosophy mirrors the way in which personal spirituality takes us out of religious systems. Philosophy is the rational, thinking aspect of your path. It is the considered way in which you make sense of the world and your place in it, working out how to live. That feeling of the numinous described in the last section is precious indeed, but to draw it into your life, that life must have the right shape. Once you have asked the vital question 'what inspires me?' you begin to underpin felt experience with reasoned philosophy.

How we balance thinking and feeling is wholly individual. Many of us lean more towards one than the other, and there is no optimal balance to achieve. There is no reason to try to seek some 'perfect' parallel between the thinking and feeling sides of your spirituality. If you are predominantly a thinking person and your emotional resonance is all around intellectual discovery, then that is going to shape your path. If you are mostly an emotional being and find excessive analysis depressing, that again will inform what you do. Humans are thinking and feeling creatures. We need both aspects, to some degree, in our lives. Our spirituality is no different in this regard. In reality none of us will be entirely lacking in one aspect. Part of the work, if you feel yourself to be a more extreme case, is to start spotting and recognizing the times and places where the other comes into play so that you can work with it more deliberately.

Every aspect of our lives is based on choice. We may talk

about instinct and spontaneity to negate that impression or we may like to tell ourselves there was only one reasonable solution. Even so these are all choices, and there are always alternatives. In action and passivity, interpretation of data, representation of self... it is all too easy to be oblivious to the choices that shape our days. We choose what we think about, what we dwell on and what we ignore. The implications are vast as these choices define our emotional experiences. Subsequent choices will be rooted in almost invisible decisions over what to think about. Every time we default to what is normal, expected or habitual, we quietly reject a whole universe of other possibilities. The more we think about everything, the more conscious and deliberate we can be. Then we have more power, freedom and responsibility. I didn't come up with this; I borrowed it from the Existentialists, and have seen a similar approach in Zen thinking.

Partly this is all about rediscovering the inner child: that former person who was free from assumption, who wanted to know how, and what and why. We are taught to stop doing that 'because it just is', and 'because I said so'. Ideas like 'because you must' and 'because everyone else does it this way' steal our choices from us. We can reclaim them. It is subversive and rebellious to ask questions. It is intrinsically a refusal to accept the status quo as obviously right and self explanatory. Once you start questioning, anything and everyone can be challenged. Nothing is taken for granted. Rational thinking can then cut swathes through the superstitious mumbo-jumbo of politics, capitalism, formal religions and all other aspects of culture as well. This is not an activity for the faint hearted! It can be frightening to realise that everything could be different, or to explore what would happen if we let go of culturally ingrained beliefs. It is also an example of the way in which we cling to belief for comfort and often prefer blind faith in systems to the consequences of daring to challenge them.

Ask who you are and what you want. Keep asking, day after

day, and pay attention to your own responses. Ask what really makes you happy and what leeches the good stuff out of life. Dare to ask what would make the world a better place and what your part in that could be. Ask how to tell right from wrong, how to judge others and how to act fairly. The only person who can give you answers, is yourself.

Learning always leads to more questions. The cry of 'but why?' can seem maddening at times. Of course it is easier not to ask, and not to think about it. The person who does not question is not free though, but vulnerable to any glib excuse or flimsy justification thrown their way. The person who does not seek to understand cannot hope to make informed decisions. Blind faith leads to blind guesses, and random outcomes.

There is more to know than a lifetime of dedicated study could hope to scratch the surface of. In choosing what to ask, we choose the path we will walk. I don't think it matters what you set out to understand so long as you make a point of thinking and questioning. Do not unconsciously choose to be someone else's unvalued pawn. Do not abdicate your power and responsibility for the illusion of ease and comfort. Think. Ask questions.

When intellect and emotion are brought together, the consequences are dramatic. We are thinking and feeling beings. To be fully spiritual we have to be alive to all aspects of ourselves. If you have rejected conventional religious structures, you have already questioned, doubted and made a choice. This is merely the beginning of your work. It is not a one-off thing, where you ask the questions once and move on, all done and dusted. Any decent philosophy is a work in progress, flexible enough to accept new evidence and ready to adapt as circumstances change, but substantial enough to help you make sense of life.

Part of the trick to making your own path effective, is to hold that flexibility. If you replace external systems with equally rigid internal ones, there's a lot of work for little gain. Of course there is no requirement to go forth and reinvent the wheel, slowly and laboriously. The world has a great many philosophical systems in it, which can be investigated and used, in whole or in part. The process of studying approaches that don't quite suit you can be excellent for pinning down your own ideas. Some borrowing can speed and ease your journey. Every idea humans have explored is fair game for your consideration and use. As with religion, the important thing is to avoid placing blind faith in the total integrity of any one system. There is no one true way, and human thinking is invariably more flawed and more situation-specific than it claims to be. Ask if ideas you encounter make sense to you and whether they can be meaningfully applied to your life. Ask what you can do with them. Try using things to see what happens, but keep your relationship with ideas as flexible as you can. They are just ideas, after all, not ultimate truths.

Spirituality without Certainty

When you get down to it, the idea of there being one, ultimate and unassailable truth is wholly irrational. Science shows us many theories, all interlinking. Usefulness often depends on scale. A useful idea for considering cells may not be of much relevance when thinking about human behaviour. Simplicity may be appealing, but that doesn't make it dependable or useful. Those who claim certainty for atheism or the dependability of contemporary science seem to me as misguided as religious fundamentalists proffering human stories as the literal word of God. There are things science is no good at, and that atheism has yet to figure out how to provide. What we have are stories, some better founded than others, but none of them totally and utterly right and none of them able to do all of the jobs we need them to perform. What we need, are multiple stories. We need science for how bodies work and all other such material questions, and we need spirituality and philosophy to help us figure out what to do with that knowledge about the material world – to help us work out how to live.

A brief glance at the nature and history of science shows us a work in progress. Theories evolve and may eventually be abandoned. All science is theory and hypothesis, tested to varying degrees of satisfaction. There is only evidence and probability, there can never be ultimate proof, and that's a key part of how science works. It's also frequently overlooked by those who pay lip service to the idea of science (as though it was a religion) without understanding it. A degree of doubt is essential to a rational outlook. With new evidence, anything we think we know could turn out to be wrong, or wide of the mark. As soon as you cling to belief in 'facts' or 'proof' you have stepped away from rational exploration into dogmatism and fundamentalism. True science simply doesn't do this. Where belief in the unassailable rightness of modern science exists, it is an embarrassing kind of dogmatism and indicates those spouting it do not grasp what science is or how it functions.

All religion is guesswork and any divine inspiration in the mix will have been mediated by flawed humans. The trouble with formal religious systems is that to some extent they all claim to have Truth. My only dogma is that there can be no one true way, and I've yet to see any convincing argument that there is. The atheists come closest to having a good argument there, but it's almost impossible to provide good evidence of anything not actually existing. You can't demonstrate that you weren't looking the wrong way at the time, that your tools are foolproof or that the failure to find evidence is not purely human. Atheism touches on something science is not able to do. We can use science to establish what does happen, and from there exclude other possibilities. We can use science to expose fakes, and understand mechanics. It won't prove there isn't a giant spaghetti monster, it cannot demonstrate that enlightenment doesn't exist and it can only tell us what happens to our bodies after death and assume implications for consciousness. There are limits.

Assuming the divine exists, the very nature of the concept puts it beyond what humans experience. Even if you subscribe to the idea of deity within, that's going to be a fragment, not the whole thing. Should we have glimpses, there is no reason to assume we have seen the whole. Human minds are finite and cannot, therefore, be reasonably expected to encompass the infinite. The whole point of gods is that they are supposed to be bigger, wiser and more powerful than us. How arrogant to then imagine we might fully grasp what such an entity wants? Or to think we can be confident about having perceived it or identified its definite absence?

To say, 'I see no evidence for God and therefore I do not believe in God,' is a line I take no issue with. To say, 'I see no evidence for God and therefore there is no God,' is significantly different as an outlook. The first perspective allows an atheist to hold their own perception whilst having room to let other people go their own way. The second version leads to hours of internet time arguing back and forth between equally rigid positions. There is a God. There is no God. I am right. You are wrong. It's very, very boring and achieves nothing.

Considering the other side of the argument… If we accept the notion of deity, we must also accept a sense of mystery and of not knowing. We need doubt and caution so that we guard against putting our own ideas into the mouths of gods and then granting said ideas an authority they do not merit. It may not be a coincidence that, frequently, those who claim with greatest vigour to know what their deity wants are also those most keen to torment and kill other humans for not conforming. In stepping back from systems and certainty, we stop giving ourselves permission to abuse.

If we do not believe in gods, that too needs holding lightly. If stridently held non-belief is seen as an excuse to harangue and denigrate harmless faith, it is hardly any more enlightened than any other excuse to pick on people. When we abandon systems, we have the opportunity to abandon all the detritus that goes with them. We do not need to be sanctimonious or holier than thou. We do not need to be more right than everyone else, or to try to make people accept our Truth. If we can embrace doubt, 'our way' is a work in progress, not hard fact, and the only viable certainty becomes uncertainty. Even then, why be too hard on the people who are certain, if they aren't actually hurting anyone? It's always possible they are the ones who got it right. I think it unlikely any human could ever be right about the nature of reality in an ultimate sense, but I won't discount the possibility that someone will figure it out.

Uncertainty is incredibly liberating. It doesn't demand that we try to convert anyone, and it doesn't load a person up with things to feel angry about. We don't have to be affronted by what other people do and think, so long as they aren't harming anyone else. It's a lot more straightforward, being affronted by injustice and cruelty, than by the ideas inside other people's heads, especially if you feel any kind of responsibility to act on how you feel. Uncertainty allows us to explore widely, to trust personal experience, reject authority, be pragmatic and flex when we need to. Not having anything that must be clung to as a certainty, we are free to let go of whatever doesn't work. This is at heart a rational response to life, and one that enables us to better appreciate and enjoy the idea of mystery. If other people don't see it that way, it's not our problem.

We are surrounded by mystery. Life and consciousness are mysteries. Death is a mystery. As soon as we try to fit the many mysteries into tidy little stories, we strip the numinous from them. Facing the enormity of all that we do not know, is a far more exciting proposition. The implications of this are vast and get a section in their own right later on.

It is worth noting that anyone can engage uncertainly with any existing religious system. If you are able to recognise the flawed, human aspect of the stories, rules and practice then you can see a formal religion as another work in progress, another human experiment in living and thinking. From that position you can explore without compromising your doubt. Whether you choose to share that openly and how other people involved in the religion may respond are other issues entirely and fall outside the remit of this book. It will probably vary a lot.

If aspects of a formal religion inspire you, then those aspects can be worked with. A person can walk their own path within an existing religion, and do so with great integrity. It is possible to participate in the most firmly established, monotheistic faiths from a place of gentle doubt. I've seen a number of Christians take up this path, unable to uphold the idea of superiority built into the system, wanting to explore more widely and be less dogmatic. The fresh vision, openness and tolerance of those who walk their own path inside a system that tries to demand obedience, is incredible to behold.

It is easy to see religions as inert systems, but in reality they grow and change over time. Without delving deeper, you will see only the face a system wears at the moment, not its history of changing. There are reasons why such systems do not invite attention to the history of their own shifts. Today's one true way is frequently much removed from the one true way carried forth in the same name a thousand years ago. Once you acknowledge that religious structures can and do change, all suggestion of their divine perfection must be called into question. The influence of people, politics and immediate need are clearly visible in the histories of all religions. If they were only ever expressions of the divine, what need would there be to ever change them? It is precisely the human aspects that create change. If we can take this onboard and hold religious systems more lightly, recognising them as ideas and traditions, not hard truths, they can become more human and more compassionate as well as being more practically functional.

Rational Religion

One of the points on which many people struggle with conventional religion, is the whole belief issue. The very essence of most faith systems is a belief in that for which no evidence exists. This is the thing atheists of course take most issue with. Any religions claiming the existence of God as self evident are a problem to those for whom the absence of God is equally self evident. Without certainty, neither position is sustainable. If you know that you do not know, opinions held as belief are a lot less offensive. The core of rationality is doubt. It is in the act of questioning and the process of seeking evidence that true rationality is expressed. Trying to convert other people is in many ways an act founded on deep insecurity. If your truths were self evident, no conversion effort would be required, but religious truths are never self evident. Only if everyone believes as you do can the essential uncertainty be masked. This is defensive behaviour, and destructive. Accepting a lack of certainty allows us to be at peace with each other and more honest about the human condition.

There is no inherent contradiction between a spiritual approach to life, and rationality. The tools of rational thinking can be applied to spiritual life. We can ask what works for us, experimenting with practice and experience. There are psychological and social aspects to religion, and a rational consideration of those can serve us well. Religions provide frames of reference, social support and social contact, all of which can be considered when developing our own approaches. Considering the real world implications of religions also raises issues around the advantages of not being a solitary practitioner. More on that later.

There are a number of existing religions that do not call for much belief. In Taoism, the ultimate power in the universe is the great flow that is the universe. Paganism and other nature based paths simply recognise that without nature, we would be stuffed. The earth turns; we need the sun; water is vital. Venerating these things as spiritual as well as physical forces doesn't call for much belief at all. Animist perspectives highlight the wonder of life itself. You do not need much belief to adore and worship life or to hold it sacred, you don't even need to believe in anything beyond this world for that position to make sense.

There is one thing a rational approach tends to suggest, which is that petitioning for help is probably meaningless. Perhaps the most irrational feature of religion is the idea that infinite, all powerful, all knowing beings will be interested in the petty concerns of our lives. Why would eternal and vastly powerful beings care about whether we get the job, date or holiday we are hankering after? Why should they want to respond to such trivia? All evidence suggests that if deity exists, most of the time it/they have no interest in what humans want. Children starve to death. Adults kill each other over sacred sites. Money and earthly riches flow towards the grasping and exploitative and the meek don't inherit much at all.

If prayer eases your mind, acts as a meditation or has some other discernible use to you, then that's a real effect and why not use it? The one thing prayer will not do is provide a solution to every ill. Rational spirituality has to accept that spirituality is not something to do to solve personal problems or avoid the normal trials of living. There are no magical shortcuts. Spiritual practice can help us develop the inner reserves to tackle our challenges and to make sense of them, but it won't make them go away. If there are Gods, they clearly aren't the uber-parents of the old style belief systems. We know that doesn't work. However, we can reject what is manifestly irrational without throwing away spirituality as a whole. We can pray in the hopes of hearing something, rather than out of the desire to be heard.

Once we relinquish the desire to have life made easy by supernatural intervention, what remains? Quite simply, our relationship with everyone and everything else. Spirituality is not a means to an end, but an approach to living. It informs not our expectations, but our intentions. If we choose to see life as sacred, the planet as worthy of reverence or the universe, time, energy or anything else we encounter as a focus of spirituality, our behaviour changes. We think and act in new ways and we re-imagine our place in the world. The divine right to use as we see fit has to go away at this point, we are no more special than anything else. At the same time, everything is precious.

There are perhaps a number of approaches a person can take to responding spiritually to normal reality, but broadly they will lead us in the same direction. When life is imbued with spiritual potential, everything we do matters. If our temple is the place we live or work, if nature is our sacred text and compassion our scripture, we deal in reality. Everything we do can become a manifestation of our spirituality. With attention focused on the real, what we do is bound to have real effects. Be it a greener way of working, peace activism or the changes we make to our home, we do not have to believe or imagine that rational spirituality achieves something. We know it does. We can see ourselves doing it. Other people will be able to see it too, and so the sphere of influence extends.

The only element of faith here involves deciding you think the material world has some innate worth or meaning and that life is precious. We do currently have just the one planet on which life depends, and time does seem to flow in a certain way. There is no more logical reason to attach meaning to any of this, than not to, aside from one critical consideration. Imagining that every-thing is pointless, meaningless and random is not a happy way to live. Choosing to see life as beautiful, and full of opportunities to do good and meaningful things is a lot more rewarding. When it comes to making rational choices, I'll pick the uplifting one over the depressing one every time, all other things being equal.

Finding Your Own Meaning

I touched before on the existentialist idea that there is no external source that can supply us with meaning. There is only the meaning we choose to make for ourselves. When finding your own path, the idea of your own meaning is an inevitable part of the process, as it is often an unwillingness to accept other people's meanings that brings us to walk an individual path in the first place. However, if we choose to accept an existing set of ideas, we are choosing them, it is no less a personal application of meaning to the world we experience. All guesses at the ultimate answer to life, the universe and everything, are just guesses. Douglas Adams's 'forty-two' is as likely as anything else and raises the important point that it was a silly sort of question in the first place. Any accurate answer might be too vast to express in a meaningful way, or even comprehended. Any reduction is a step away from truth.

My personal feeling is that the universe exists as an answer to the question of life, the universe, and everything, and that the enormity, vast beyond all imagining, is both the only ultimate truth available, and totally beyond real comprehension.

If we intend to make our own meaning, we have at least deliberately chosen to think about things rather than going through life with the usual cobbled together amalgam of barely relevant ideas. Absorbing carelessly leaves us vulnerable. Governments, for example, might like us to believe that the meaning of our lives is wealth creation and that we exist to serve GDP. Religions tend to place meaning in the hands of largely unknowable gods, served by our making said religion and its leaders wealthier. Of course there's a grand plan, we just don't know what it is. To improve the lot of others may seem meaningful, but if we all did that, where would the 'others' come from? Companies sell us 'meaningful' lives in the shape of having the right clothes, home, body shape and so forth. Adverts tell us regularly that if we haven't got the right products our lives will be meaningless puddles of misery.

The meaning we accept informs what we do. If we've absorbed that unconsciously, we could be in all sorts of trouble, as with the above examples. If you've become a good little consumer and wage slave by absorbing the meaning-messages of government and producers, life is not happy. It's not meant to be happy, it's meant by this measure, to be useful to someone else. If the only meaningful thing you can see is material wealth, then accumulation of an ever greater hoard becomes your work. There is no point of sufficiency with a hoard, and no point of achieving satisfaction with such a belief system. At the other extreme, total dedication to service can overwhelm you with the enormity of all that needs doing and the total impossibility of sorting it all out. Even if you set aside all personal gain to end wars, save starving orphans and halt extinction, you've still got to clean up the oceans and re-freeze the ice caps.

Thinking of meaning on such individual terms can be problematic, although the path of one may suggest we do just that. Having a sense of fitting into a bigger scheme, being one positive force amongst many, is a lot easier to live with. No matter how solitary your path, when it comes to the quest for meaning it is useful to remember that other people are doing it too, and it's not your sole responsibility to sort everything out. You do what you can, no one can do more than that.

It may seem easier to do away with meaning entirely, pottering thoughtlessly from one event to the next with no grand plan. However, it is the desire for meaning that draws many people towards the spiritual life in the first place. Once you start asking 'why?' and 'what is it for?' it's very hard to un-think these questions. It is the asking of the unanswerable that takes us out of just existing from one day to the next. There is so much that cannot be settled by rational means alone. Why are we here?

What are we supposed to be doing? What is it for? The absence of answers creates an existential crisis. This is an alarming thing, and not always a welcome prospect. The certainty of religion only works to distract from this if you can mange not to question it.

The rational human is a questioning creature. The incessant 'why?' of the inner child takes us head on into the unanswerable, the impossible, and the profound discomfort of not knowing.

We live our lives with no real certainty about what said life means or how to even live it well. I think for some of us, that uncertainty is far more unsettling than the certainty of eventual death. We cannot have answers to the most important questions, and no matter how disquieting we find it, the only thing to do is face the not-knowing, and accept it.

In not having answers but asking the questions anyway, we bring ourselves to the absolute reality of what it is to be alive. Gaze upon death, try to imagine eternity, consider the mystery of consciousness, ponder infinity and the small flicker of our existence looks small indeed. Yet at the same time it is also the brightest and most miraculous thing that we exist at all.

I think we have to keep asking what it means. Why am I here? What is the purpose of my life? How should I live? It's not a quest for one tidy, reassuring answer so we never have to worry about it again. It's a work in progress. Giving up systems and religion means giving up on tidy answers in search of something more real. We have to keep coming back to the rock face of existential crisis, in all its enormity, and keep asking. If we can live with all the intensity, awareness and determination we can muster, we can live that answerless quest for meaning from one day to the next.

I don't think answers are available (aside from the beautifully simple and utterly useless forty-two). However, by a slow process of attrition, I see the things that are not answers. No amount of material wealth will help me when I stand before the unknowable. No amount of worldly power or fame seems to make any odds to it either. I can hide it from myself with distractions if I want to, but I can't make it go away. Every time I face the mystery, and the enormity of it and ask 'why?' I chip a little bit off myself. Some tiny grain that was irrelevant falls away. I get a fraction less involved with all the things that clearly were not answers. Perhaps by this means, some solution to the existential crisis might ultimately be possible. I do not know. Perhaps death will teach me. Perhaps it won't. I just keep coming back to the rock face, asking what it means, and trying to keep my life as free as I can from the things I know are not the answers.

My theory, for now, is that the point and purpose of life is to try to understand that which is inevitably beyond us. For me, all else flows from that. Even so, it's just another way of phrasing the question, not an actual answer.

Intrinsic Paganism

Where Paganism offers religious structure, it is as capable of coming up with dogma and rigid thinking as any other faith. The absence of a central text does not stop a minority of Pagans from announcing they too have the One True Way. Those who crave power and authority will do what such people have always done in response to spiritual community – they try to harness it for their own advantage. Where Paganism functions as a formal system; able to exclude and dictate, it is much the same as any other system. Practitioners of Paganism can be told what to practice, how to go about it properly, in the right gear, and how to feel. Thankfully, most of my experience of Paganism has not been like that. For the greater part, Pagans are fiercely independent and take pride in not being easily led. Many people who self identify as Pagan are walking their own path, and simply find aspects of ancient Paganism and modern reinterpretations pleasing and resonant, and like to have connection with fellow seekers without having to conform to anything much. Plenty of Pagan groups have minimal structure and are inherently flexible, working more by sharing what occurs to individuals than by trying to force everyone into the same shape of thinking and feeling.

The idea of innate Paganism is something that gets a fair amount of discussion within the community. Innate or intrinsic Paganism is that which bubbles up from our relationship with the land, as an innately human response to being alive. Things which crop up across cultures and times – festivals of light at midwinter for example – are often taken as examples of innate Paganism shining through. However, the idea of intrinsic Paganism can be a bit woolly, running close to empty words like 'instinctive' and 'spontaneous'. These can be re-postulated as 'stuff we do automatically without thinking about it'. It pays to give this some proper thought.

Not everything we do on autopilot is intrinsic Paganism or even intrinsically human. We can be trained to responses we are not aware of, through adverts, social conditioning and the habits of those around us, to name a few more obvious influences. If we salivate in response to something that isn't food, that's more likely training than nature. Saluting automatically is the product of training. Much of the behaviour we might ascribe to nature or instinct (almost everything around gender identity for example) is just as likely a function of the culture we live in. The way in which different cultures and periods have constructed gender identity is a good example of just how natural this aspect of self isn't. So much of what it means to be male or female, gay, straight or other depends on your time and place. Some of the gender experience is rooted in the physicality of our own bodies, but far more stems from how society teaches us to think about those bodies in the first place.

It's only human. It's natural. It's normal.

There's a great swathe of justifications around 'instinct' that need to be explored and understood before we can start looking for intrinsic Paganism. That everyone does a thing does not make it inevitable, natural, or necessary. I refer you to the wearing of corsets and the binding of feet. We ended slavery, but in its heyday, that was viewed by those who liked it as being an unavoidable part of the natural order. We ended the divine right of kings, and that used to be unassailable. We're relinquishing the idea that gayness is somehow unnatural. It often takes a longer view across history or culture to get many aspects of human behaviour into context. Those individuals who like the status quo will use 'normal for now' as a measuring stick as though the freak circumstance of the moment represents a rule, or something we should aspire to. Anything that can vary across times and places is not a hard fact, just something we happen to be doing. Most things that humans do can be done in many ways, or not done at all.

As we step away from systems, it becomes necessary to question the very language of nature and normality, and consider how that language is used. Is it perfectly natural to kill an unfaithful partner? That's a classic excuse for murder. Is it the natural way of things that might is right, and only the best should survive? Is it natural to select out the weak ones and leave them to die? The political consequences of how we apply the words 'normal' and 'natural', are vast. We use normal as a measure of acceptability, abnormal as a word of criticism. We've deployed normal in a way that implies normal and natural are the same thing. Variance and diversity are more natural than homogeny, and in many ways, healthier.

What is it in your nature to do? How can you tell what is intrinsic to yourself, and what is a consequence of a lifetime's social conditioning? Is it even meaningful to think of human nature as separate from the context in which it occurs? Can we be anything other than the products of time and place? How much of who we are really is inevitable, and beyond our control? The more we ascribe to nature, or to culture, the less free will we assume ourselves to have. The nature/nurture debate may have raged for a long time, but when do we start asking what role there is for free will and choice? Do we have to be products of our biology and circumstance or can we choose to reject that? Obviously there are things we can't choose to have different. I can't be taller, I have this body and the options it brings, but I can choose how to deploy it. I can reject ideas and I can try to identify and break social conditioning and ancestral habits. Without this perspective, I could not function as I do, but so many people act out of training and assumptions about who they are without seeming able to even question that at all.

When we seek to strip away systems, blind faith and complacency in the quest for genuine spirituality, what are we looking for instead? I think the critical thing here is that it must be something more immediate. Something more real, personal and affecting. As we stand at the rock face of existential crisis, we can start to add more personal questions to the list of things to shout. Who am I? How much of what I want and feel is really me? How do I tell the difference?

Cognitive Behavioural Therapy and Zen philosophy alike will teach us that our thoughts are illusions and the drama of life and self are fantasies we create. Animism and pantheism both take us towards ideas of spirit or god being present within us. Some faiths paint humanity as lowly sinners in need of redemption while other paths will tell us we are good enough already. Are we natural, or unnatural? Should we seek to be immersed in nature, or to transcend it? We don't really know.

We have nature, both externally in all that is around us, and in the immediate experience of our own bodies. We have tribe and family, culture and country all telling us stories that shape and define us, but at the same time this can smother us in layers until we no longer know who or what we really are.

To some degree, the spiritual journey is a quest for self. Mainstream religions will tell you the exact opposite. Be it striving for Nirvana or total submission to the will of Allah, mainstream religions abound with methods to lose yourself in something greater. Why? I think it confers the benefit of silencing those most alarming questions: Who am I? What am I? Why am I? If we can rest, literally or imaginatively in the soothing, annihilating embrace of deity, that questioning voice can be made to shut up for a while. Perhaps forever. Of course, if you're an atheist, that's not available. Perhaps the mantra of 'it's all biology and none of it means anything' has the same soothing influence for some. If the voice of ego, or self, or inner child does not want to shut up and stop bothering you, then you will have an ongoing fight inside your head. Is the answer to 'who am I?' really to try to annihilate the voice that seeks to ask the question in the first place? What would be the point in that? Surely, the ease of not asking is just another illusion we spin for ourselves?

If we aren't asking who we are, it becomes much easier to tell us who to be. If we aren't peeling back layers of training to expose the voice of self, we can build up more layers and assumption and conditioning. We can of course seek the comfort of silencing ourselves, if we want to.

What if that little questioning voice is the voice of spirit? What if this is the god within, or your innate nature speaking? This could be your guardian angel, your higher self, or any number of other things. We don't know, but that shouldn't devalue it. Comprehend it as you will. What if that questioning voice is not there to be pacified and subdued, but to keep us wide eyed and alive from one moment to the next? The closer we can get to uncovering our own natures, the clearer our perceptions of everything, within and without, should become. Only with total honesty, and some attempt to explore our innate selves, might we be able to really think about what comes naturally. What is our natural response to the manifold experiences of being alive? Where is our innate spirituality? What does our rawest and most essential self show us? Starting from even an attempt to discover the natural self we have a better chance at working out what innate Paganism might look like. The spirituality that rises up as a truly natural consequence of being alive, and being human, is unfettered by systems of power. It may be natural to want comfort, but the degree to which we've abdicated power and identity to achieve it seems irrational to me, not natural. I have no idea what truly innate Paganism would look like, but suspect it would be simple, happy and not constantly putting us at odds with nature or our natural selves.

In looking for innately Pagan ways we can go back to that idea of spirituality as a felt thing. What do we feel? What inspires us? Joseph Campbell says, 'Follow your bliss,' but to do that you need to figure out who you are and what your bliss is. I rather think the two go together, that our natures and our great loves are in many ways the same thing, and that in enacting one we must inevitably reach towards the other. We are what we do, what we think, how we live and we are everything we feel. When we do the things that feel most right to us, we also feel most like ourselves. There is a cyclical process here, one all too easily taken the other way. If we do that which feels wrong and we become less like ourselves and less able to see what our right path would be and so forth until all is confusion and unhappiness. Our culture tells us to go after the money, the status and the shiny life, regardless of nature, and in a desire to be who we are told we should be, we stop being who we are.

A spiritual person is looking for their bliss, their inspiration and place in the world. Thus they are looking for themselves.

Community without Dogma

One of the functions of formal religion is to create and reinforce community. In terms of the real world effects religions have, this is one of the most important considerations. It can affect those involved on a day-to-day basis, shaping their lives far beyond the more obvious influence of belief. The social aspects also serve to reinforce belief through shared upholding of behaviour, and can tacitly enforce compliance through peer pressure even if no sanctions are available for non-participation. Thus there is a feedback loop between community and religion which helps to hold the individual inside the religious system. If deviation from the religious system means social exile, many people simply won't consider it an option, even if no direct punishments would result. For much of history, religious structures have gone alongside community structures. The fragmentation of modern life is a recent development, that has loosened the bonds for some, and served to make the structure even more important to others.

The affirming of social identity and a participation in a social group is a big draw for people, and may have little to do with actual belief. The breadth of religious communities can also have interesting implications. Most social activities tend to keep us with other people of similar age, wealth, education level and life stage, while religions have more capacity to bring in a broader spectrum. Religion can remove barriers to social integration and can build bridges between different segments of a populous. They can also entrench difference and emphasise distance.

Atheism does not have a viable alternative to offer, as yet. Without being able to replace the social function of religion, there are places atheism and agnosticism cannot go. The absence of text hasn't created much in the way of songs to sing, rituals to attend or wisdom to share, and this prevents atheism, as it currently exists, from offering a social alternative to religion. While the real-world influence of a system remains attractive, there is reason to engage with it, even if you have no faith. Regardless of what we believe, the social functions of formal religions are very attractive, and set up to be with us at the most dramatic moments of life change, too. Most particularly, religions offer a social framework. We know when to turn up, how to behave, what to wear, what to say and around that exists a safe space in which we might interact with other humans. You don't need to be socially adept, you just need to know what the rules are. It's very seductive.

Secular culture offers the gym and the pub, which cannot begin to compete. There are many special interest leisure groups, but they exclude more than they include. We can't all find our solace in amateur dramatics or flower arranging, nor would we all want to. The net result of abandoning formal religion seems to be ever more isolated individuals who depend increasingly on televisions for an illusion of social cohesion. Soap operas become our neighbourhoods and watching gives us something to talk about at work. The Gods of the small screen may attract more worshippers than the various temples, but we're certainly no better off for that. Arguably, it is a harmful development. We don't know the people around us. We don't participate in their lives and we do not care about them. Depression is on the increase.

We are supposed to be social animals. We evolved to co-operate and live in groups. Moving away from community comes at a heavy price, emotionally, psychologically and practically. Community in the UK used to be all about the church, as would be true a lot of other places. For hundreds of years, the church was the social centre of English life (alongside the pub, admit-tedly). It was the one place everyone showed up to regardless of age, wealth or anything else with the power to individualise. We've largely given that up, but we haven't replaced it. People need communities. Many of us have voted with our feet, escaping from the restrictive rules and dogma of religion, but that leaves us with nowhere, physically, to go and connect with other people. The shopping mall and cinema complex don't provide a meaningful alternative. We don't want to be lectured, to utter formulaic prayers and mumble through familiar songs. We do not want to sit in obedient silence and listen as the man at the front tells us what to think and feel. You can have that bit just as well with your television anyway.

The trouble with making your own path, is the absence of obvious fellow travellers to share it with. The temple of one offers no community. There's no one to run your rites of passage, or support you through a crisis of faith. No one to lend you a useful book or invite you to a friendly prayer circle. There aren't even any coffee mornings. You could go out and evangelise to collect your own followers, but this would be a bit of a betrayal of the ideal of a personal path. You're just a new potential system, not a rejection of systems, at that point. So you're left with the problem of not having any songs to mumble through in a vaguely sociable way, and no time at which to show up somewhere. This is as much an issue for atheists as it is for people on their own path. The most dependable virtues of organised religion are social, and those are the hardest features to replicate if you don't like systems.

History isn't much help if you're looking for alternatives. The only cultures not underpinned by religious systems seem to have philosophy or political dedication in the same niche, working in the same way. When you look at what actually happens to people living under it, there's disturbingly little difference between fundamentalist regimes, and communism. The songs may be different, but the controlling intention is exactly the same.

So far this chapter may sound a bit like a litany of doom and gloom, but there is a model out there that does seem to work. Pagan moots (essentially social gatherings) open circles and open rituals are surprisingly diverse in their membership. Many Pagans identify as 'own path' anyway, and mostly do things their own way. They will engage with moots for the social and community aspect, not with any desire to conform to something. While you do get the odd (very odd) Pagan who craves order and authority, most Pagans are not interested in converting people and have only academic interest in what the next Pagan believes. Conversion attempts are not considered socially acceptable in Pagan groups, while comparing experience is common practice. Thus the loose framework of 'Paganism' offers a safe space in which a rather disparate set of people are able to meet, share and connect.

This loose community can even function for ritual and rites of passage. There are Pagan, Christian, Animist, Atheist, and Polytheist Druids. Stand in a Druid ritual circle and the odds of the next Druid seeing the world in the exact way you do, are actually rather small. As a consequence, we have to do rituals without assuming too much about what anyone else believes. We tend to make spaces where everyone can speak for themselves. The shared bits of ritual are more about celebration and common values – social justice, green issues, aware and responsible living and creativity, alongside recognition of the changing seasons and the natural world. It works.

You don't actually need rules, dogma or a hymn sheet to have a functional spiritual community. What you do need, is a place and time to meet up and some hope of finding commonality. There usually is common ground – we are all human, and all seeking something. It may be that the seeking is a more productive binding influence than the idea of all having found the same thing.

For the solitary quester, the own-path person who wants a community, I can say only this: Make one. If you haven't found a place where you fit, create it and see who else turns up. Mostly all you need is a time and a place, and some willingness to take the risk that no one else be interested. It is surprisingly easy to start a community and to find like-minded people. It is also worth considering moots and Druid circles. There's little risk of anyone trying to convert you, and the rituals tend to include cake. You could even try looking for fellow travellers at church coffee mornings and the like. I've found a lot of churches in the UK are so starved of attendees that being a Christian is no longer a critical requirement. Many Christians are open minded enough to talk, and if you find dogma, you can always leave and try another place. Questing for spirituality can also require questing for the right space to do it in and people to share it with. Spirituality is human, and humans are social beings after all. While some people are solitary in their spiritual pursuits, many of us crave contact and a space in which to share. Know who you are and know what you need, then you can act accordingly.

Giving up the systems does not mean we have to give up on everyone who is still working within them. Formal religions tend to have the spaces and the cake. If the isolation of solitary spirituality bothers you, going and having a debate with the religious people can be a good antidote. The intellectual and social stimulus can be helpful, while you will get reminders of why you wanted your own path in the first place.

Stories and Texts

The Great Book is a central feature of most mainstream religions, although notably absent from both Shinto and many variations of Paganism out there. Aside from core texts, most religions have a large canon of accepted literature you can turn to, safe in the knowledge that it will keep you in the system. As a lone practitioner you don't automatically get issued with a book (not even this one, which I rather assume you wouldn't want if there was any suggestion that you had to read it...). While this might seem like a disadvantage, it's quite the reverse. No one fixed book means that you can choose from everything out there, or reject everything, or write your own.

There's not a lot to be discussed around the idea of rejecting core books outright. You don't need a book to be a spiritual person, after all. Spirituality appears to pre-date writing, our cave-painting ancestors seemed to do fine without texts. A book cannot turn you into anything, although it might contain useful pointers. Books pin things down, they turn fluid ideas into hard statements, and that may be a reason to reject them. Authoring can smack of authority, and writing your own book creates the temptation of trying to get someone else to read it. If the idea of spiritual books seems wrong to you, then don't have one, and consider skipping ahead to the next section.

You may consider writing your own spiritual book. This can be approached in a number of ways – collecting things you like or making the whole thing up from scratch. Poetry, prose, little wisdom statements, stories, anecdotes... all forms of writing are yours to play with and you might choose to focus on a few, or just throw in a bit of everything. You might want to do it with an eye to sharing or it could be wholly private.

Your other option is to explore texts from other religions and philosophies to see what you like. This may give you more of a pick-n-mix approach. You may also find that, once stripped of their accompanying systems, religious books that can interpreted freely are much more useful things. You might also choose to range more widely in the quest for wisdom.

Generally, books central to religions are not just about spiritual matters, and this is an interesting consideration. Most religious books contain social and political aspects. There may well be elements of actual history, or an attempt at creating a mythic history of the world that served as history when we didn't have as much science. Stories of founders dance between history and myth, but come with a considerable helping of what the religion wishes you to understand about how it wants to have begun. Vast systems of belief and practice can build up around the interpretation of what are, in essence, a selection of stories. These same evolving systems also inform the story-making process. Most ancient holy books were not written in a single, inspired burst by one person. Most are amassed over time from various sources. The choice of what to add or include, and what to exclude has everything to do with power and authority. The decisions that shaped The Bible as we now know it deliberately excluded a great many texts because they didn't fit someone's vision. On top of this, the process of translation into new languages, and as languages themselves evolve and change, will shift meaning. To give a non-religious example, many people take 'wherefore art thou Romeo,' as meaning 'where are you, Romeo?' when actually it's better translated as 'why are you Romeo?' with reference to the problem his family name causes Juliet. Languages evolve, understandings change, and what we do with our classic texts undergoes subtle shifts that can distort everything. Messages of peace become justifications of war.

If you make your own book, then you are both authority and audience. The only risk here is of creating a new dogma for yourself. Words on a page, if over-valued, can inhibit growth and change. We are learning as an ongoing process, so today's brilliant insight can turn into tomorrow's face-palm instigator. Writing it down can encourage us to cling to things rather than holding them lightly.

The recorded word can also be a very useful tool, and the flip side of the argument has much benefit to offer. The act of writing can be a good way of refining and crystallizing ideas. The element of inner focus in such a process is useful, and in getting something straight enough to write down, you may push towards coherence more effectively. Recording what you think as you go along can leave you with an interesting history of your development. The embarrassment of early writing is, in any context, a useful antidote to self importance. The act of making a spiritual book can become a good focus for your spiritual life, but it could equally turn into an unwelcome distraction. There is no one true way, after all. If writing seems to be a good idea, then it probably is.

Collecting together useful thoughts other people have come up with can spare us from laboriously re-inventing the wheel. I think there are some excellent one-liners ascribed to Jesus, and I borrow them shamelessly. You may have noted occasional pilfering from Joseph Campbell, Douglas Adams and others as well. I'm like a magpie, and I'll lift anything bright and shiny that catches my eye. I do even look to more Pagan sources as well. Greeks and Romans are also subject to occasional pillaging. I happen to like the mediaeval Welsh stories that probably aren't ancient Paganism in the raw, but speak nonetheless to a lot of modern Druids. These tales might contain grains of Celtic myths, but no one knows which bits those are. I like the stories and they make sense to me, and so I draw inspiration from them. But why stop there? Why only draw on what is old or established? Age can give the illusion of validity, but ideas need to stand or fall on their own merit. If we become sceptical of authority, what reason is there to assume the authority associated with age really means anything at all?

Religious stories are basically just stories. They may be old, influential or laden with cultural baggage. They may have a bit of truth or history in the mix, but even so the odds are that somebody made them up. Perhaps other people down the years embellished them for good measure. If we can strip away the claims to authority based on divine inspiration, what we are left with is a bunch of influential stories written by people.

Any story has the potential to inspire a religious experience. If the experience of reading moves us, if the story reveals something meaningful, uplifts us or makes us aware of something we had not previously considered, it may have also functioned as a religious text for us. Who created it, when and why are of far less personal significance. It's only that we tend to give more time and attention to the 'right' books and feel less silly claiming inspiration from them. However, a thing does not have to be made with spiritual intent to have a spiritual effect. Here's a good moment to nod to the many people who put 'Jedi' as their religion in the last UK census. I'm sure for many, it was a joke, but perhaps not for all. And why not? If Yoda and Obi-Wan Kenobi best express how you want your relationship with the world to be, why not claim Jedi as your path? One of the Druid Orders – Berengaria – works specifically with the wisdom of science fiction and fantasy. I've long felt that Terry Pratchett offers one of the best introductions to practical witchcraft you can find, and Douglas Adams remains one of my favourite philosophers. A good story is a good story and through them we tell each other who we are, what life means, and what it's all about.

One of the joys of giving up on conventional systems is the freedom to recognise inspiration wherever you find it, and to run with whatever makes sense to you. No one else has to agree, or approve, or even understand. If what clarifies your decision-making is asking what Gandalf would do, that's as good a tool as any other. We can pit ourselves against any story, asking what we would, or would not do in that scenario. It's all just human creativity, human inspiration and human life. What more could anyone really need?

No Ethical Guidelines

One of the great complaints from people of book religions about independent spirituality, is the absence of rules. You are free to pick and choose, and therefore it is often assumed you just do as you please with no standards or regard for others. Considering the ways in which religious texts are appropriated to justify anything and everything, there are clearly no guarantees that claiming a set moral framework will reliably result in behaviour everyone else might approve of. Even within religions, debates about meaning and application vary. A religiously derived moral framework is really speaking about something to turn to for ideas, and it does not follow that in rejecting religious structure you have rejected honour.

The way in which some people would like to prioritise a morality based on religion would have more weight if anyone actually adhered to it. The vast majority of people who self identify as faithful do not uphold every rule and guideline their religion has to offer. Often there are conflicting messages anyway. As a Christian for example you might feel entitled to stone adulterers, or you could take the line 'let he who is without sin cast the first stone' and decide that you aren't entitled to go that way after all. Rules about not killing are set aside for wars all the time. Guidelines suggesting charity and compassion are not reliably upheld.

One of the big problems with rules is that no matter how nuanced you make them, life will throw up situations that defy easy solutions. People are also very good at finding excuses for why this one time, what they did made perfect sense. Most of life's challenges are not tidy, and the rights and wrongs are not easy to pin down. When we're determined to see ourselves as right, we'll bend reality to fit, we'll reinterpret, re-imagine, downright lie to ourselves if need be, to keep that feeling of rightness. All those divorced people who think gay marriage is a threat to the institution of marriage, spring to mind as prime examples of bending reality to fit your agenda. Imagining that the rules came from God does not keep us on the straight and narrow. It doesn't reliably lead to better behaviour, greater compassion or wiser judgments. People who mean to go their own way aren't swayed much by rules, they just tend to work out why, in their special case, it shouldn't apply. Of course sometimes the rules themselves are too crude and the situation too complex to simply apply what was in the book. At which point no matter what we came to a situation with, it is our own, individual judgment that defines what we do.

There are a lot of reasons why humans of the 21st century are outright rejecting the rules of book religions. There are cycles that are both created by and informing of this process. The change in female status is an important example. The move away from treating women as second rate and innately sinful brings a lot of other attitudes and beliefs into question. Rising political power and rights for women has undermined the rules and assumptions of traditional religions, and as people continue to move away from religions as sources of all wisdom, that empowerment process is improved. The same thing is happening for gay and lesbian people too, and for Pagans. That which was once demeaned now flourishes, and everything else must change in response. Those who have historically been stigmatised by religion are increasingly able to flee its influence, and the flow away from sources of oppression and bigotry are visible in some places. At the same time, fear and poverty combine to create a flow in the opposite direction as well, towards fundamentalism and intolerance. There's a real tension here. Those of us who are tolerant may want to tolerate the intolerant amongst us, but whether that will work out well remains to be seen.

The world is a strange, uncertain place, and the desire for an illusion of security can lead people towards fundamentalism.

Clinging to rules, to ideas about the right way to live, and refusing to flex can be one way of making yourself deaf to the voice of your own fear. This is in essence what fundamentalism is all about – convincing yourself that you have the answers and do not need to be afraid any more. The more fundamentalist a person is in their views, the more fear they probably have; fear that they cannot acknowledge and have to try to hide from themselves. Only by accepting doubt and uncertainty can we make some kind of peace with this fear and be free from it. As it is fear that motivates fundamentalism, we won't make that kind of cruel rigidity go away by frightening further the people who cling to it. Anything that threatens a fundamentalist serves to reinforce their beliefs.

There can be all sorts of reasons that prompt people to move away from old values and moral systems. People with a desire to transgress (by religious standards) have every reason to throw away the rulebook. One of the things that religions offer us and people increasingly reject, is the idea of sins against God. Actions that arguably harm no one and that are arguably natural, can become unacceptable simply because the religion has designated them that way. There are many of these taboos around sexual behaviour, as previously observed. Intolerance of masturbation comes to mind as an example. Masturbation really doesn't harm anyone, and reduces sexual tension in a way that might actually reduce sexual aggression, it's about the safest form of sex you can get, and ironically enough offers a substitute for all those other sexual sins religions disapprove of! Where contraception is a sin against God, women are locked into cycles of birthing and all too often burying babies. I could go on as there are many such examples. The intolerance created by ideas of sin can seem woefully lacking in compassion, especially if you view the sin as a human construct, not as something issuing from the divine. Where religions control behaviour for the good of society – discouraging violence for example – there's an easy case to make for utility and value. However, when the sin is against God, and nothing of this world suffers, serious questions need to be asked.

The idea of sin can often seem like an expression of prejudice and a rejection of much that is joyful in the physical world. Sins can also be about a failure to show up at religious places, make appropriate payments to the religious functionaries, and can be a consequence of not accepting the word of religious authorities as law. Again there's a relationship with authority here. Rules express authority. The person who has the power to make, interpret or enforce rules has power over you, and I for one find that inherently objectionable in matters of spirituality.

Spiritual laws about who we are allowed to love, and what kind of love is offensive to deity trouble me. Not least because the net result is so often the control of women and their fertility. I raise again the issue of entirely human stories being foisted upon the world as divine truths, for the purpose of benefiting the few at the expense of the many.

Rules around clothing, fasting, celebrating, and others governing harmless human behaviour have distinct functions. Such rules make it easy to assess submission. If you look right and act right, you are behaving as required, and under control. If you accept being told how to behave in these regards, you will be more open to further acts of control. Dress codes and behaviour rules can give an impression of community and social cohesion. Such rules make it easy to spot outsiders. They can also turn practitioners into vulnerable minorities. Conformity serves abuse from both within and without, and there is every reason to be wary of it.

If you want to make someone obey orders, starting with relatively easy and trivial things breaks them in gently. Religious rules all too easily become tools for control in the hands of tyrants. Cults often develop ever more complex and demanding rules, taking the convert deeper into a place of being controlled, which sometimes leads all the way to death. When we learn to follow instructions too well, the price can be very high indeed.

To accept unquestioningly the rules derived from religious books is often to accept that you are seeing the will of God laid out in those books. The idea of divine will can make it possible for people to accept practices which make no sense, or are actively harmful to them. This is not an option if you maintain a questioning mind. If you need to understand what the point is, you are less likely to be manipulated. You can believe in deity and still find the idea that minor tweaks to costume and behaviour will please the divine, or that minor deviations from the rules will make divinity angry with you – totally illogical. Why would supreme beings be so petty? It is people who like the uniforms and conformity of underlings, and people who imagine that preference onto deities.

Religious rules and systems change over time. The emphasis can shift, and most practices evolve. The Hindu caste system did not pop into existence fully formed. The shrine rituals of Shinto vary from place to place. Every religion contains examples of change, many have branches that are orthodox and others that identify as modern and more radical. Every major religion is full of subsets and splinters, each with its own focus and interpretation. They cannot all be right if there is only one true way. If we consider them all right to some degree, we are accepting that these are just human best guesses. We are then free to acknowledge that religious rules are made by humans, for entirely human purposes. This is not about the will of gods, or the business of pleasing gods. We can keep or discard ideas based solely on whether they work for us.

What if you don't want to start from a sacred book in order to figure out how to live? The whole history of philosophy is there if you want a different system, but it is possible to start from scratch. As with the idea of building your own philosophy, you can build your own ethical principles by questioning, considering and experimenting. In practice, this is what a lot of people who appear not to have formal guidelines are doing. To be without externally defined rules is not to be without honour.

The tools I've found most useful for thinking about ethics, I borrowed from a book on Existentialism, which read so long ago that I cannot name the author. It might have been Sartre. This approach doesn't give any answers, but helps to formulate useful questions and ways of thinking. The first method is to consider that in your words and deeds you are demonstrating to everyone around you how you would like the world to be. If you then recognise that you are not in fact acting in the way you think the world should be, that might prompt the making of changes.

If you are trying to determine a course of action or consider the consequences of a behaviour, ask yourself two questions. What would happen if everybody did this? If the idea of everyone doing it seems fine, then that's a good measure of reasonableness, as you'd also consider it OK to have this done to you, or around you. Ask also what would happen if nobody did it, as that is often a productive counterbalance to the first question. It might, for example, strike you as being bad news for the species if everyone was gay (or good news for the future of the planet). If no one was gay, we would lose out in terms of human diversity. The balance suggests to me, that there needs to be room for both gayness and straightness. However, all this method can do is reflect back something of your own pre-existing values. If I hated homosexuality as a concept, I would see no one being gay as an excellent thing, and everyone doing it as a total disaster and measure accordingly. The one thing this method does, is helps to clarify thinking and to steer you clear of hypocrisy. It pays to pause and ask why we think the outcomes would take a certain shape, rather than letting personal assumptions go unchallenged.

These kinds of assessments can be used to place any choices I make within a spectrum of possibilities, and I find this helpful. Often by imagining a different scale for our issues, by imaginatively universalising them, they make more sense. It is not viable, I have to note, for everyone in the world to be a professional author, but the world would seem poorer to me if there were no professional authors at all. Amateur creativity is a splendid thing, but allowing people the time to dedicate enables much greater achievement, which in turn brings greater pleasure and insight to others. Once you start poking about in this way, all sorts of knock-on effects and wider considerations can come into play. Everything we do has consequences, good and ill, depending on how you view them. What is success for the fox is tragedy for the rabbit, after all. Not that I believe that all things can only be judged relatively. We can be absolute in our condemnation of that which we find wholly unacceptable, if we so choose. In my case, it is cruelty that I find invariably unacceptable. I can consider reasons that might make a person feel some act of violence was necessary, but cruelty is never needed, it is all about the sadistic pleasure of the perpetrator. As that pleasure is not necessary, I find it unjustifiable. There are plenty of inoffensive ways to vent sadistic streaks. Many fiction authors manage it, for example, through the deliberate torture of wholly imaginary people.

There is a whole world of difference between following externally set rules and living by your own rules. A person may avoid crime or sin due to fearing the consequences should they be caught. In that context, said person might readily do everything they thought they could get away with. If the only crime you believe is an issue is the one that gets you caught, you'll only uphold the rules when you think someone else could notice. Those who behave in fear of punishment will not necessarily behave once the fear goes away. If you believe that really it's all about power, or opportunity, then if you gain power you will use it.

The person who acts based on their own conclusions will act consistently, know what they are doing, and know why they are doing it. The person who believes in the choices they have made is much more able to live an ethical life than the person who merely does what they are told. Ethics are about choices. If we have no choices, or have them taken from us, we are not able to act ethically. Religious rules therefore can be as much a barrier to an ethical life as a form of assistance.

We are better off when we challenge ourselves to find our own way. Or as the Wiccans put it… an it harm none, do what you will. Which once you start to think about it, turns out to be a pleasingly complex proposition.

More Than Lip Service

A person of religion who goes along with all the forms and instructions is not automatically also a spiritual person. Such an individual may have the surface appearance of religiosity, but this is not meaningful. To be anything other than theatre, a religion has to be lived. It must be thought and felt, acted upon, and intrinsic to all things. The alternative is just lip service and social conformity. There may be a point to that, but it isn't a spiritual one.

Anyone who wants to engage meaningfully with a religion has to go through a comparable process to the person who discovers and invents their own way. Everything has to be questioned and considered. A personal relationship is needed with the books, rules, costumes and meeting places.

Religions all breed heretics and dissenters. There are always those who insist on coming to their own understanding of the truth, and who will not put their blind faith at the disposal of other human beings. No matter what deity they honour, the modern heretics seem to be an exciting bunch, open to other people's truths and able to think clearly about the system they still identify with. Many heretics of my encountering have been heartfelt in the practice and full of integrity. Then there are the other ones who throw away authority not in search of independence, but out of a desire to be in charge. They hasten off to start new ways of worshipping, and if needs be, whole new religions just so that they can head them up. It is not hard to spot the differences between a person who walks their own path and a person who wishes to pose upon a pedestal. The first will be doing something, the second will be much busier demanding your attention.

If all the people who came to formal religion did so with a questioning mindset, religions would cease to function as power bases and potential tools of oppression. We're back to the issue of what happens when we try to calm our unavoidable fears by getting someone else to tell us what to do. We buy an illusion of safety at a high price, all too often. While we won't deal with the fear and acknowledge it, the pretence of a way out remains all too tempting. No religion can give us certainty, which is why all too often what people do when they engage with religions, is to get into complex activities that enable them to forget the fear for a while.

On the other side of this issue, it is important to acknowledge there is much beauty and heritage associated with the major world faiths. The inspiration of faith has prompted many stunning creations. The financial power of religious bodies has commissioned many beautiful artistic expressions across all forms of human creativity. That legacy remains, in buildings, art, music, in our museums and in books. If we can be flexible in our thinking we can reject what obviously comes to us from historical human failure, keep the good bits (as we subjectively identify them) and move on.

The odds of any own-path person coming up with a spirituality that has nothing in common with anything else, are small. We are all connected by story and history, and by the realities of living and dying as human beings. Whatever truths we arrive at will likely have common ground with other people's truths. The point isn't to try to come up with the wildest possible innovation, but to develop a spirituality that you understand, believe, and are interested in. To do this it is necessary to explore your own nature and your relationship with everything else. It's not enough to get the ideas straight as an intellectual process, either. The only meaningful spirituality is lived as an intrinsic part of your life. The rest is just posturing, image creation and leisure pursuit. If your aim is to dress up and be applauded, become an actor or a model instead.

Where we throw off the systems of religion, it is not faith in deity that we necessarily abandon. Only faith in those humans who claim to speak for deity and who want to tell us what to do, needs to be given up. The person who is devoted to their own path has no place in their spiritual life for either authority or subservience. There are simply other people to connect with, where learning and teaching can be exchanged in fluid ways. It is not necessary to give up the things you love in order to walk your own path. It is necessary to relinquish some certainty, and all of the bullshit.

Religious systems can beguile us with promises of comfort, a good spot for the afterlife, divine favour and peace of mind. The offered bribes tend not to manifest, and when we put faith in the bribes, we abandon our common sense and self determination. We none of us know what happens after death, but this life is discernibly real to us and we owe it to ourselves to do the best we can with it. To which end we must each decide what 'best' means, and be willing to refine or redefine that if we need to as we progress.

The vague suggestion of how to create a path in this book offers little by way of ease and comfort. It will take you to the existential crisis and it won't tell you how to feel good about it. If we use our rational minds, we know that stories to make the fear go away are just stories, not truth. The only truth is that we cannot answer the big questions, and it comes down to each of us, in the loneliness of our own minds, to face up to that and choose what to do as a consequence. There are no definitively right answers. There may be a wrong one though – to delude ourselves. All we ever really do, is choose. We can try to do so consciously and try to choose well.

A Better Life

Part of the point of religions is clearly that they offer to give you a better life, in this world and when you die. However, formal religion will also tell you outright that this isn't the point at all. You aren't supposed to be enjoying yourself or sorting out your petty human woes, you are submitting to a greater thing, as defined by the religion. Your work is to obey the religion's ideas, transcend the flesh, escape the cycles of rebirth, submit to God, or some other comparable activity. Once you get in there, many religions are clear that they do not exist to make you happy in this life. Some religions at various times have sold their methods as solutions to life on earth as well though, with material power and practical gain very much on the agenda. Many religions tell you that life is awful but that you can collect points towards a much better afterlife to make up for it all. That idea may make suffering in this life easier to bear. Equally, the idea of a grand plan in which what we endure means something after all, may make the realities of living and dying easier to cope with. Again, these are simply ways of hiding our fear from ourselves. Nothing is actually solved or improved.

Most people come to religions because they want something, and that, 'something' is not to submit to the actual will of an actual God. The following list probably isn't exhaustive, but I think it covers most of the major motivations.

- Desire for political and material power and wealth.
- To have status, importance and respect.
- Wanting a sense of belonging.
- Hope.
- The desire to be a better person.
- The desire to be able to feel better about yourself.
- Wishing to become educated.

- Wanting to be wise or enlightened.
- Wanting God on your side.
- Wanting marvellous superpowers.
- Wanting to feel secure.
- Wanting to have our problems solved and to be told it will all be fine.
- Wanting someone else to take responsibility for us and tell us how to live.
- Wanting to feel loved.

In short, we want it good and easy, we want to be important and loved unconditionally and religions give us that – at least in theory.

Religions do tell us we can have this, and at the same time tell us that we shouldn't be focusing on it because there are more important things to do. The contradictions around the better life versus life of service are fascinating. It is the quest for the better life which draws us in, but it is the methodology of serving with no hope of anything better now, that actually creates a lot of the problems in religious systems.

I don't think any of this is an accident. Religions are a subset of the stories we make up and tell to each other. If a story is to do more than pass the time, it must tackle a need. Religions are the stories we tell in answer to our fears, to make an existential crisis go away, to silence the terror and help us feel better about ourselves, our lives and inevitable sufferings and demises. We also imagine fiery pits of unenlightened doom for our enemies, in smug certainty that the gods do not love *them* at all.

We come to both region and spirituality because we want something. It might be a small and innocent desire to feel better. It may be the halo glow of the saint, recognition of our martyrdom, or a really spangly title. The vision of becoming the High Arch Super Guru calls to some of us. In claiming the spiritual life we can play out our most infantile ego games whilst pretending to be better than everyone else. There are times when I look around at the titles, pomp and self importance and really question if a spiritual life is even possible. Here I am, touting my own wisdom and importance by writing a book, pausing only to polish my halo. How do I tell that I'm not just doing all of this so that I can imagine I'm more than I really am? Self denial can become the most sensual of pleasures, as can pain and suffering. Ask any BDSM lifestyler. Sacrifice can be all about self importance, and the quest for enlightenment can be a tool with which to weave ever larger webs of fantasy around ourselves.

This in itself raises unnerving questions about what we do and how to trust ourselves. I run into this one every time I put myself forward. Am I just kidding myself? Are my motives good enough? Does it matter what drives me? Would I be any less spiritual if it came down to a desire to feel loved? I go back, every time, to that which is human. It is human to be afraid, and uncertain, and to wish that the universe loved you. It is not the aim of spirituality to somehow become something that is not human. However flawed I may imagine myself to be, I am unequivocally human, my urges are human, and it is precisely that flawed, urge-laden humanity that sets us seeking spirituality in the first place. If we were perfect and had all the answers, we wouldn't need it.

Our brief, uncertain existences are challenging and we all get a large helping of pain and distress along the way. Of course we want life to be better. By 'better' we usually mean easier and more comfortable, and more coherent. This brings us right back to the rock face of existential crisis because religions cannot make our most fundamental problems go away. We will suffer and die and we don't know what comes next, if anything. What we want – actual security and comfort – is denied to us by the very nature of life itself.

We can build own-path spirituality as a way of pretending that all will be well in the end (which of course it might be, who knows?). Or we can hold our doubts and fears, recognise what we most long for and try to make it ourselves. That which we want to find in our lives, we mostly have to put there. If you want wonder, you have to go out into the world ready to feel it. The best way to reliably feel love is through bestowing it on others. The most dependably real experiences available to us are created by our own actions. In the giving of comfort, the giving of hope purpose and resonance, we also make something for ourselves.

Yes, spirituality can give you a better life, but only if you go out there and create it. To do that, you need to understand what you want and not be looking to any external source to hand that over to you. All the stories about how it could be are just idle entertainment if we do not set out to make them real. Spirituality is lived, breath to breath and choice to choice, with all the awareness we can muster. Anything else that we merely claim to do in the name of religion but do not live, is make-believe and self deception. It doesn't matter what you call it, or in whose name we do it, only that we live our belief rather than waiting for everything we want to be given to us.

It's a question of flow. Formal religions describe a flow between human and the divine, with worship on our side and being divine on the other. We want love and good things to flow towards us and make life better. That's not reliably available. I therefore postulate that to live a meaningful spiritual life and feel good about yourself, you need to make a flow that goes the other way: From the self, outwards.

The world we attempt to create for others, we also create for ourselves. If we speak and act with integrity, make works of beauty, love widely and give of ourselves, some of that will likely be reflected back to us. Even when it isn't, some faith in the integrity of how you live can elevate the most grinding and mundane of efforts into significance. Opening the heart to loving others; be that people, places, creatures or ideas, we feel love more directly than when we bask in the glow of love returned. In living your understanding of what life means, living your ideas about how it could be, you make that, to at least some degree, real. Not for the sake of Gods who might or might not exist do we do these things. Not to save up for a deluxe afterlife that may not be available. Not to appease or impress, but to act out the soul truth of who you are and what you want. It doesn't take a lot of belief to live this way. The results of living your path are rapid and real. Unlike most of the alternatives, it does work in measurable ways.

There can be Gods, in this understanding of how to approach spirituality. There can equally be no Gods at all. There can be a spiritual essence to the universe, or just mechanistic process. It doesn't matter, because the focus shifts to how you live and what you do. Let the rest of reality take care of itself. There's no gain in arguing or fighting over the unknowable. Lived spirituality is real.

Endnotes

1. http://www.guardian.co.uk/news/datablog/2012/dec/11/census-2011-religion-race-education
2. *The Power of Myth*, Joseph Campbell

Moon Books invites you to begin or deepen your encounter with Paganism, in all its rich, creative, flourishing forms.